It Starts as a Seed

Kevin Sarkisian

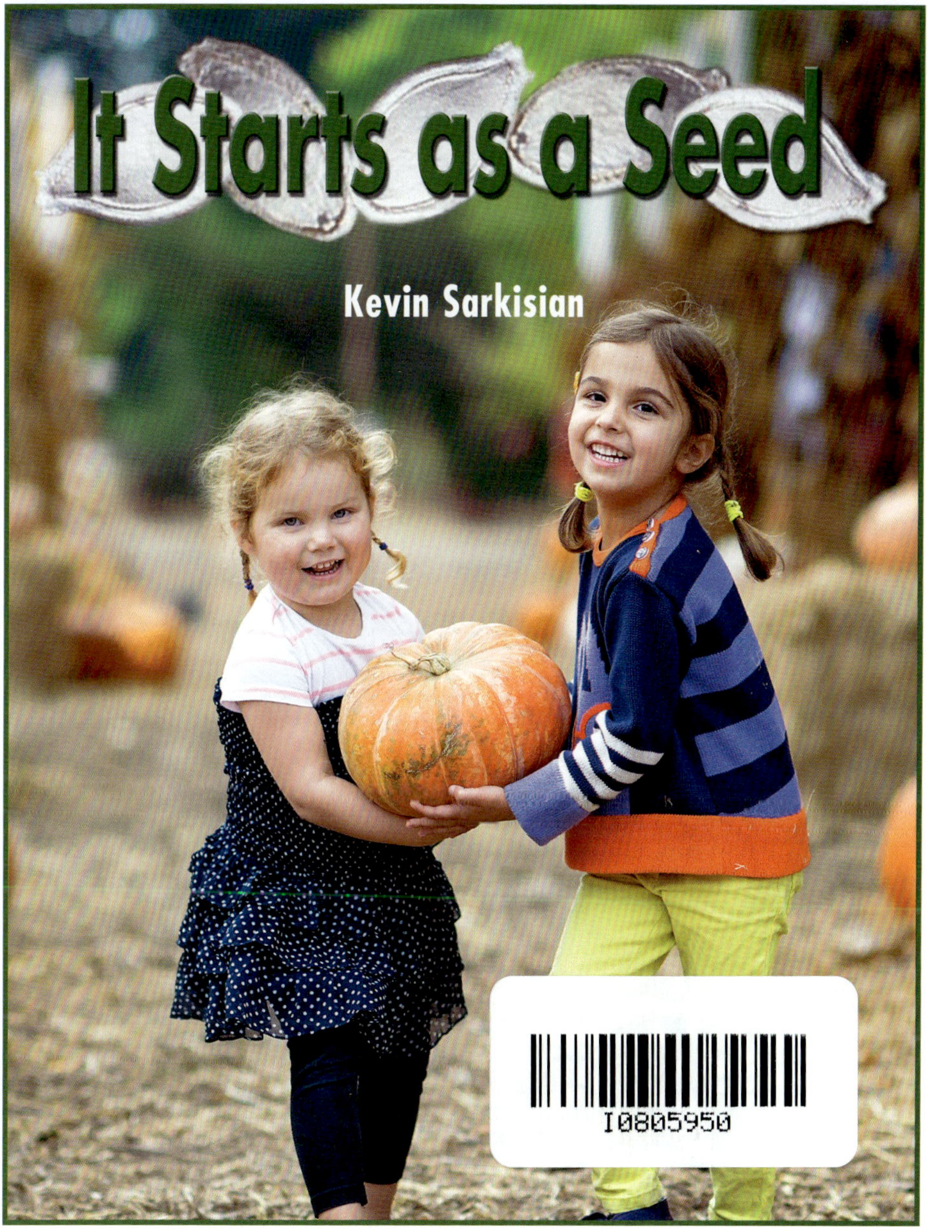

Rosen REAL READERS

Rosen Classroom Books & Materials
New York

Pumpkins start as seeds.

We put the seeds in the ground.

The seeds need water to grow.

The seeds need the Sun
to grow.

First the seeds grow into plants.

Then pumpkins grow on the plants.

Words to Know

ground

plants

pumpkins

seeds